the best estimation in the world

THE BEST
ESTIMATION
in the world

(By)   Sonia Farmer

POINCIANA PAPER PRESS

Published by Poinciana Paper Press
Nassau, The Bahamas

ISBN: 978-0-9989150-2-9

Copyright © 2019 Sonia Farmer

No part of this book can be reproduced in any form
without permission in writing from the publisher

Book design by Sonia Farmer

Cover designed and letterpress-printed by Sonia Farmer
in a first run limited edition of 300 copies

Cover graphic used under license from Shutterstock.com

The documentary will be late.

– As per my last email, circa 2015

FEATURING

THE OVERALL RECORD FOR BEING HUMAN
(This Is Not) An Interview with the President and CEO   3

THE HOMESIDE EXCURSIONS
(This Is Not) An Interview with the Senior Vice President of Finance   11

THREATS, PRACTICES AND OFFERINGS OF THE HIGHEST STANDARD
(This Is Not) An Interview with the Senior Vice President of Administration and External Affairs   17

TODAY IS OUR MISSION
(This Is Not) An Interview with the Lead Designer   23

OPEN AND LEARN TO BE RELEASED
(This Is Not) An Interview with the Core Works Director   31

ARE PEOPLE STILL OUT THERE
(This Is Not) An Interview with the Non-Core Works Director   37

OUR DUEL ROLE CALL
(This Is Not) An Interview with the Managing Director of Critical Paths for Operations   43

NOW THAT I CHANGE
(This Is Not) An Interview with the Creative Arts Director   49

THE BLACK LINING
(This Is Not) An Interview with the Chief Marketing Officer   57

THE DISTANCE GENERATED BY A KNEE
(This Is Not) An Interview with the Chief Operating Officer   63

THE OUTER FRINGE OF A GOOD THING
69 *(This Is Not)* An Interview with the Area Vice President of Lifestyle Hospitality

A SECRET FOR SERVICE
75 *(This Is Not)* An Interview with the Director of the Academy

DO NOT RISK THE LOCATION OF THE SOLUTION
81 *(This Is Not)* An Interview with the Executive Director of Leadership Development

BECOMING THE CANDIDATE
89 *(This Is Not)* An Interview with the Managing Director of Luxury

SIT DOWN AND TRY TO BE SOMEONE
95 *(This Is Not)* An Interview with the Interior Designer

THE DAY YOU GET TO CLUTCH
101 *(This Is Not)* An Interview with the Vice President of Human Resources

A HOMICIDE WE ALL KNOW WELL
107 *(This Is Not)* An Interview with the Corporate Director of Destination Marketing

THE REST OF OUR LIFE IS NOT A POEM
115 *(This Is Not)* An Interview with the Front Office Manager

your dream job is here

THE OVERALL RECORD
FOR BEING HUMAN

(This Is Not)   An Interview with the President and Chief Executive Officer

1

memory is a profitable process

I believe you are looking for an investor
to come into your heart
a destination
with three thousand rooms

I'll eat your worries
the constant threat
of our notorious end

we need this feast of injury
to design a home run

the original massacre
that concept is still the same
what changes is
our costume

showered with my godly intention
I'll roll us into stars

so join me in this dance
to the brink of morality
without a visa
to return

2

this is my home now

with such natural beauty
in a great location of recklessness
we are able to hear the devil

it's been a while
he says
ask me to make out

on your knees
you are my own thing

damn
we are pretty
who will join us on the coast
to take communion

line up here
and leave your names
and children
in the sand
for the waves to suck away

3

whenever your dream doesn't like you
pursue it and eventually you'll get it

we took this the area
as a clean sheet

starting from scratch
the scenic water was
just a trickle
now this country is a web search
threatening our showcase to the world

everything we won
is right here
the tourists
still new in their plastic box
I was lucky to find them
back in China

I think it's alive
the potential of this country

by that I mean
we've created the dawn
in a city of unknown energy
and lease out this miracle
behind God's back

4

the departure of flies
out of some late whale
has inspired me

would you be interested
in a resort
where the government
privatized the dead

we were thinking of building
the brand
inside their mouths
once the renovation is complete
they will be more friendly

when everything in the government
is commissioned
I win over and over again
and you will too

you know
it's not just about the scheme
it's about our worship

if you buy more residences
you'll have a stronger connection
to all of us believers here
and our anthem of fireworks
helping us to make guesses
about the scenery below

5

come see our people
full of comfortable horror
and mediocrity

little more than chances
we built our home
where we had to

in the morning
we serve our moral reaching
as a well-rounded meal

we go to work
with other orphans
and enjoy all the greetings
of the barbarous heat

at the end of every day
we always return
to this very narrow
breadth of understanding
we call home
and call out to
beautiful mythical places
in prayer

tossing all of the sweet
things that inspire us
into the salty and ruinous air

6

what do you believe in
here in the life of service

everybody is a push pin
it's really all about
hanging on

people cry
with their heart beating

such lazy legitimacy

I was there at the end of it
when the nail
split our brains

we get to keep the world
when we go

this room which we dream of
every time we die
does not change

it's no wonder
you would like to scream

poor innocent
never give up
that's a lesson

this hammer belongs to us

when our guests come
to this same old room
let's see
what they believe

this hammer belongs to us

THE HOMESIDE EXCURSIONS

(This Is Not)   An Interview with the Senior Vice President of Finance

1

my mouth
is a major economic undertaking
I know what to say
to make things happen

I studied accounting
and then went to work on recruits
just for your kind of holiday trip

we estimated our budget
to the size of the body
visitors love
to go down on the summer

the destination
has been announced

this region
is on casino time
and in place
on the Chinese calender

people will buy tickets to see
this great anywhere else

2

since we entered
into construction
job creation is still adjusting

the government's
given us the concessions

for every dollar
given this conception
they will earn
some human perspective

we're calling it
a duty-free kind of killing

it's the color
of the great recession
this optical shop
fluent
in our national identity

3

I bought the rights
to keep smiling
through hundreds of private meetings

do whatever to testify on TV
find opportunity in a towel

the country has its own duty

I could feel the IMF
standing outside the confines

peel apart
the concrete walls
slice the skin of the gross
domestic product
and scoop out
the payroll dollars

once you do this
you'll find out how people agree
to another foreign investor
dropping anchor here

4

the city you're thinking of
is really just some sentiment
behind a poster

we did our best
to try to act as a nation
that they have time
to change
but we're an economic collapse
and still each year
we choose to run this course

the GDP
is really just a measure of
how pathetic the country becomes
over a period of time

we're going at the speed of
billions of dollars

what we are now
is a huge toy
passed island to island
the next version
of our enduring homelessness

5

I think when you're free
you don't get to see
your home destroyed

it's never really
a different scenario

you know
all said and done
I'll miss
reading the horizon

others can tell you
the story
maybe hundreds of new
talented people

I'm just an accountant
jumping
out the window
seeking duty exemptions on
some sort of relief
breaking the ground on
a new country

THREATS, PRACTICES AND OFFERINGS OF THE HIGHEST STANDARD

(This Is Not) An Interview with the Senior Vice President of Administration and External Affairs

1

my career is coming
full circle once again
and I find that
extremely encouraging

over the years
we've seen the ups and downs
hotels on Cable Beach endure

I've experienced
every one of them

creating unemployment
from multiple endings
we were able to navigate
those disappointments
put in place strategies
that will make us stronger

I'm so privileged to be part
of this last resort
continuing my career
as one of those iconic
ghosts of tourism

2

I put it on ice
our cemetery of icons

we have to get past
the whole idea of tears
all mourning a hotel on a beach

only the biggest budget
can lean in close
with the whiff of
that same objective
and the challenges that taste
of the western hemisphere

we'll make these spaces
behave in public

we didn't call demolishing
we don't watch
the country fall

we called it
the renaissance of tourism
the rest is history

3

as a custodian of history
I am in a good position
introduce the same set of hotel plans
through ownership changes

to train this team every day
we tell them
of things to come

be prepared to accept it

I have to educate the public
break their necks to watch
this project grow out of the ground

the foliage we open
for individuals seeking
to look up from a few cards
is really a must see

4

don't let
economic growth in this country
cost the benefits of this country

look at the racetrack
all the tinsel
gambled away

I miss
the whole of the last forty years

we were little then
knowing nothing of
the expectations of freedom

excellence in tourism
took place on paper
but the development of it
required salt on the renovation

the poachers
answered those calls
with their Cinderella fairytale
hostility

5

to participate in the gutter
you need to commit
to exploits

my jacket is on
for the last show

the Chinese government
sponsored the road costume
this feathered
infrastructure development

but we all
agreed to lie

who is it then
selling all that exists
in the country

offering our best
broken-backed employees of choice
to buckle under
the weight of this foundation

successful in attaining
everything we hoped for

TODAY IS OUR MISSION

(This Is Not)   An Interview with the Lead Designer

1

I have always been
the Holy Grail
my desire
crafts projects
of striking order

I am the master planner
of collective consciousness
I found
the boutique
often specializing in boutiques

pick up my name
so that you can wear it
collect out of the ether
the best of me
collect my ideas taking leave

very good
you need to celebrate beauty respectfully
let's not waste it

after all
what is talent
but opportunity

2

I suspect you'll want to hear it out
how to become successful in life

well
that can be a very tricky thing
there has to be chemistry

my boss has been around
for thousands of years
and is still relevant

I'm engaged to our pricing
and I'm really glad
that it's working out

sex is a great example
of how the creative process
can work

we needed a baby
something with an iconic look
made of concrete that greets
all of our guests as they arrive

that's how important a building is

3

I think my newfound view
is disposable

how we look at our scenery
all that is so choreographed
an old inspiration
which came from a lender

the guest experience
is not really authentic
it was placed into the project

it means something
a bit more special to me

I wanted to steal
a sense of the tropics
design a certain level of hell
that they've never
experienced before

I personally was caught up in
postmodern modernism

isn't it fun

with all those thousands of crimes
that was our year

4

we always strive to consolidate
corporate blessings

excuse the environment
we are competing for the same thing

in order for this product
to be truly authentic
we need to make this thing
sort of like the beach

even though we may be
thousands of feet
away from the beach

luckily
we collect them
coastlines

beauty so bad
everyone would have to spend millions
to create this thing

cravings so timeless and unique
you don't really have a choice
but to come back

just hoping to catch the sarcasm
that keeps design relevant

5

looking at the tragic
tremendous achievement

I wanted him to leave
the server

he could not appreciate being here
in the hallway with a sense of déjà vu
wondering what it's all worth

he ate my belief
he taught me
what I feel like

a property
that drowned publicly

the facade is so
monochromatic
a signature element
of despair

I think that's what it always comes to
sitting in this boring
typical cool place

6

something that everyone
can enjoy in the moment
is desperation

you hope that you can condemn
all the tools that you needed
to be successful
when your list of demands
become your list of debts

I personally felt
everything believable
lay within this building

it's up to me to
bury it

come inside
this is the black box experience

we broke it open
we brought the sand in
and we made our bomb

you know
the core beliefs and quirks
we're selling
are dust

now are you excited

now are you excited

OPEN AND LEARN TO BE RELEASED

(This Is Not)   An Interview with the Core Works Director

1

the casino says it's time
to earn another resort

it wants my Hollywood
movie magic
to help guests walk in the front door
and look at the beautiful view
from this wild shortcoming

the poor world tour
was the drop-down menu of choice

it's very important
to maintain the state of euphoria
around the world

sourcing a very special place
for this homage
to the distance between guest
and insular poverty

2

before
the logistical challenges here
were a lot more complicated

dreams had to come
to the Caribbean
by the translation
of stadiums overseas

to overcome these problems
we became a charity
for employees

a mix of good fun
and a number of excuses

the maturity
of this detailed planning
could knock you
off your feet

3

uniformed up
in cells on the casino floor
the poor go as planned

you know
the syndrome

if you live in captivity
you keep your nose
to the floor
for a few tossed cents

missing the light
streaming
through this wooden horse

4

honestly
we watch the place
on all fours

sick of being part
of these amusing
acts of sodomy

there is no
bailout bill of the soul

the task is now
seeing this through

please enjoy
the adventure of local exhaustion

that's what you get
world

please enjoy the adventure

ARE PEOPLE STILL OUT THERE

(This Is Not)   An Interview with the Non-Core Works Director

1

I've been doing this
for a long time
landscaping
the skin of our country

I'll decide
what needs
to be taken out
and what needs
to be preserved

fire all the buildings
I'll make three of them a day

redesign
and paint over
timely reminders of budget

I'll knock down
the money tree
until we decide what to do
with its debt
and then stitch closed
the sinkhole
for a golf course

in this arms race to win
the local economy

2

it's so important
that we continue to improve
our environment

the more local participation
the better

some of them
came out of the old hotel
we leveled

the simple local
in the holding area
we're using
will be incorporated
back into the landscape

so that we have one
continuous vision on loop
for the great outdoor show
and all of its expected wildlife

3

in paradise
we have a lot of what I call
topographical variations

some walk out of
the lobby of a tent
and look up

some walk out onto
the balcony
and look out

it's a great view
for a minute

the satisfaction
of staring in awe
at places where
you cannot stand

4

I'm opening up
our marble floor
gather your feet
and hold your breath
through the excavation
of years

we used to enjoy
the picture we constructed
in the arms
of the conqueror

but when the lost maps
start to unfold
you start seeing
more and more

it's already
a long time ago

worked to the core
I call on the edge of history
to say that I'm sorry
for the lawless things we did
in the name of archaeology

5

it's clear
a resort of this magnitude
has an environmental impact

point out a less invasive species
than typical resort guests

what do you see
from your elevation

from where we're standing
the concrete structure
hovers up in the air
like a blade

honing our longing
every single day of our lives

each year I collect another scar

we hope you
come down to visit us
sometime

OUR DUEL ROLE CALL

(This Is Not) An Interview with the Managing Director
of Critical Paths for Operations

1

we'll tell you
what your career is
at this hotel

many different instruments
make music

we need all of them
to orchestrate this masterpiece
articulating the vision
of our brand

when you are able
to serenade the door open
people will run in

their tickets
always on standby
for this intimate concert
of executions

2

understand
that for this project
to be successful
a couple of pieces
from the past
have to be included

you will need
to meet the expectations
of our appearance

our convention center
uses Botox

if we don't properly
execute our local look
we won't appear
that different from
the era for Great Britain

its freedoms
a fictional warmth
lingering from
its leftover hallmark

3

start putting
all those pieces together
and you will find it too

our home
is just a painted picture
all of us living
in the confined
frame of culture

reflecting an awful
magic mentality
we are collected
by a very gifted owner
behind the camera
focusing in
on the beautiful gardens
where we're buried

each one of us
speechless stories
somebody else
made up

4

I find that we act
as a benchmark of success
but it's not our world to play in

uniforms separate us
from the suits

processing
these two perspectives
is sometimes referred to
as a war in the wrong room

released inside it
you are so small

don't linger there
we have rules
and heavy security

it really messes up
the resort kind of feel
for everyone

nobody wants to
think about it for too long

those undocumented warriors

5

I've worked hard on stage
for my solo moment

I'm just a fiddle
in the end of its life
trying not to make
the same mistake again

let's begin
a new secret picture

throw a dollar
into the canyon
of my grave

my jaw is loaded
with the most interesting notes
to execute people
over the heat
of its delivered wonders

NOW THAT I CHANGE

(This Is Not)   An Interview with the Creative Arts Director

1

our history is an affiliation
with the heart
a hotel
with its own design
and audience

we will try to satisfy
all the moments

rearranging them
I will be responsible
for gathering props
to create exhibitions
for people to tell
different types of stories

they're going to be replicated
and duplicated
a bin of boutique hotels
I wouldn't buy

2

our present day negotiated away
this week has become an object

I've got a pretty kind of month-old history
it's very rare
the stuff I don't really think about

like we are just a moment
to roam around the hotel
and the ships

that's all ever I do

I think I'm a disgrace
people shouldn't be able
to come into our horror

we wanted great cities
packs of kids that could become folks

we are supposed to be
making art about the Bahamas
but I think that we're allowed
to disclose a more complex identity
teach people
to tell a different type of story

the service happens
when you present those ideas

3

I think we prayed for corporate souls

promoting the country
is not so easy

you know
I can be proud
I've existed mostly between
the reception area
and the casino floor

I'm nowhere
but hotels are so in touch with this life

I met with an awesome beach hotel
thank God for most of their dialogue

all of the conversations I quit
and I still talk about it you know
the kind of music that comes out in faith

don't you see
I think about every should be
now me already was

I thought I was a moment
but the mind of the statue
has been through so much demolition

I remember five minutes ago
I also remember the future

with the end I get
maybe I'm not ready for everybody to go

4

being sad about change
is no longer tolerated
don't wear it longer than a year

who we are in our history
made me
I'm no artwork
and I'm up on rest days

generally speaking
it's been a great story to create
but it exists metaphorically

we are committed
to the ongoing rotating wheel

I know
I experienced this when I was a child
did you not watch

we painted a painting
it was hard times

5

I'm so happy to know
our time and experience so far
has been disobedient

I know that you know
I don't like priorities straight and senile

we wanted to pay very close attention
to the way things would be reflected
it needed some new definitions
not legal in all your unity

it makes sense
for this space to become broken
I think this habit to start bleeding again
occupies a living will

what's this about
the crazy softness anyway
deaths should be spectacular
as big as the original painting

you will see it
opening before me
with two thousand five hundred
structures

a deep rich red
juxtaposition to God

6

I think it's something
that we really need to take seriously
when we get to see ourselves
on shore

haven't moments here scattered
we're here to speak

we can cut the history of hospitality
trip it again
and you'll see

we are the country
we are called to it
we are Jesus
and you have to give us something

I walked by the country
so what

I kind of feel like an eclipse
wiping out this development

the last play of light
the East saw
is yours

we are called to it

THE BLACK LINING

(This Is Not)   An Interview with the Chief Marketing Officer

1

it's time to wonder
how we would like you
I wish I had really started earlier

as you know
everybody has target areas
you get credit for showing minds
that are worth viewing

bring them out
the execution of a brain
lasts about a minute

I love the way I forget
the same beach
guess why we laugh all day
and start early

easy is the only destination
look in the travel magazines

that's one of the things I did
for our love

2

before we can
transform the country together
we need to want the same thing

he is our building
we all have a thing for
he is really high up there
has always been

I had to communicate more in luxury
so that's how I sang to him

he saw me
bathed in fuel

little cuties
I am the dearest
temperature

in the theme of each year
we saw a gap
we laughed and ate there
we set up our I dos
to the color of my tweets

when you think about it
without our fire
hell would be very wet

3

so many people
in his armed gang
get trained in trafficking
their free nations

I will be our house

being in love
always makes you feel welcome

from in here
we made them feel
that peace is a place

in the sophisticated arms
of the delegates
I am reminded
the real work of renovation
is forgetting all
we will make harm over

my inner self came and went
with their men armed with swords
ensuring nobody
has their say about living life
in an actual act of war

4

these days our love
has more of that TSA feel

the top of the world
is not a lot more
than a block of detainees

in line for the half life
holding a bouquet of weeds
thinking that they can wait a week
deepening the way that they die

he knew what I didn't

I had a lot of time
to be in the act
as if there is an end

what's it like
to find a country
that you get to love

live anywhere
under the thumb I know
and forgetting
will haunt you for all of your visit

the grieving process begins
after the brief falling away
of final eye contact

time for the eye unlovable
to break loyalty

5

I know the answer
to why people live
on their knees
in an amazing tropical paradise

I have been
the wife of this weight
for some time

when you steal things like
our feet
you cannot jump
from the high life

we are merely an era of draining
and the sea is a place
that will outlast the earth

he has a knife
and some change
coming in for your wife
or a thousand

worry that you'll still be here
at the end
when the dam
filled up with his
terrifying heart
trembles

THE DISTANCE GENERATED BY A KNEE

(This Is Not)   An Interview with the Chief Operating Officer

1

one's life mission
is to always ask
how can I win

in school
I worked my way up the ranks
then transitioned
to the gaming industry
and it branded me to the brim

we want people to have
the natural affinity
to be crammed into that attitude

in a resort like this
we get to understand
the value of assault
by working together

the day
a tight fist

knocking out
our chances
to be special people
sitting in a chair
by the beach

2

this country
is a Mrs
and we are in love

we're bringing in the
experience of our sin

our twelve hundred slot machines
will have fire in the room

home means to me
her arms around me
soothing and calming
my new suffering
in this world economy

bring in folks
from the inner cities
to experience
this bond too

they can't speak
looking in the eye
of the mother proxy

when you see that everyday
it's just so inspiring
to mean so much
to so many people

3

when you weren't looking
we collected
an assortment of crown jewels

everyone wants
to be a winner

within them you know
that the fire in their heart
will never make a difference

strictly focused on
immediate service
immediate action
they walk by you
aggressively hospitable

that's the spirit

we just moved this island
to tears

4

they call us
winners
but we are the people
that people care for second

I start work
so sad
at the bottom our casino hotel

when I get in
and I see the people
so young and excited
about being there
I think
why are you smiling

being executed
through the noose
of success
is an offer you can't refuse

we're all
high rollers now
going all in
on the spectacular opening
of this stolen crown

the biggest and brightest
gamble of all

why are you smiling

THE OUTER FRINGE OF A GOOD THING

(This Is Not)   An Interview with the Area Vice President of Lifestyle Hospitality

1

our farm will be a game changer
in the hospitality industry

other people might say
we were the contract
of overexcited fussiness
but this study is not a deluded
hot take

all the cells
enjoy themselves
they have come to show
an affinity for luxury
and great service
in their deep tissue

I've been designed
for such individual properties
part of my DNA
now it is stuck with me

when you attend to luxury
then sometimes
you get to be a luxury
too

2

this is a very extensive
training program

his idea of art
is really evolution raising

he came up with it
from a placemat
to make us
become the icon again
on the shore

we're looking for great character
in a bountiful person

the warmest being
says anything
out of high service

I am so grateful
that I am the owner
of this fire

you know
this is very emotional for me

I'm not necessarily saying
lucky you
because you're alive
but it really sucks
to be anyone else
within our property sentence

3

we pride ourselves in restoring
an authentic sense of discovery
prying open
the gates of Eden

we have always needed
an ear for Evangelisation

we infuse these laws
into a skull
and make the radiology
correct their flesh
so we can teach them
everything we believe

the freshness you want
in that early service
is an unpretentious
anticipatory air

beverage options
by the million

all for this nation's
discerning travelers
with all of their incomes
and their guts
to buy harm

4

just living
really is a lifestyle choice
in the hospitality industry

everything within it
is a common threat to our bodies

honestly
we're all the same person here
certain traits of a character
that work for our cartoon culture

is this really
how we look
how long do we embrace this

the answer
can't end with the problem

my dear brethren
keep the porch light on

I would like to hear
what death calls me
in the early morning hours

5

people act
like it's not so serious
this guest loyalty
becoming a quashing order
across the nation

I'm so scared of what we do
in redefining luxury
that word
within the edge of its meaning

the guests are far worse
than in all of our lasting memory

considering what we're known for
fear the worst of us

this is not
high end enough
incredible hospitality
burns

the property
on fire
is now serving

thanks for staying with us

A SECRET FOR SERVICE

(This Is Not)   An Interview with the Director of the Academy

1

we want to see your teeth

bring them in
for screening
in one-on-one interviews

the onboarding action is different
than anything you've experienced

there are some traditional elements
of the application process
and there are some
nontraditional elements

we don't recruit from just
inside of the industry
we also don't recruit
from just outside on the street

it takes a mix of folks
to make it successful

this subjective vision
to create something like
anyone has seen before

2

I know the shots

he told me some of the things
that we don't talk about here

like the bailouts after
you help the world
get out of her skirt

he had a real heart for service

since that conversation
my job is something different
every day

if he hears us talk
then we can talk about it
all the way down the skyscraper

if you like to speak
suck it up
before I step back
to shoot you down
with my hands for healing hospitality

3

very often
there's a perception
that we are hiring
particular people

to be the right fit for service
you have to be a person
who is trusted

we listen for passion
we can hear it when it's real
we can hear you get turned on
by hospitality

we are opportunities
within the country

you are
that last puzzle piece

come home and
make history

we are going to have an eye
on this industry
in this country
for a very long time

4

the audience wants it so much
our debt

when you look at a hotel
do you think about the subsidy
of this love connection

when you look at a resort
do you think about the stink
of our ongoing internal dialogue

I wanna talk about that

I wanna fill this space
with a suffocating
amount of words

until people understand
how we're made
they cannot hear
the buildings going up up up
every day
like a tremendous bit
between our teeth

going up up up

DO NOT RISK THE LOCATION OF THE SOLUTION

(This Is Not)   An Interview with the Executive Director of Leadership Development

1

we are creating
a wonderful tool bench
within reach of the sea

many of our young people
are equipped
with particular circumstances
scared to be constrained
in the eye of employment

I see my calling
to help them sit up
without a spine
and introduce them to
some golden visage
they can reach for

be the best tool
you can be

the most top pencil box

with the right talent
you can earn
two tickets to discover
our noted prison
and train
with the highest expectations
of defeated obedience

2

with its power
the audience is of course
a very critical component
of our training

to be quite honest
we didn't know what to expect

but when the spark was set up
the fire
exceeded our expectations

now everyone wants to stop
and appreciate the intensity of
this concert of bulbs
trading from the very moment
of their conception
all individual thinking

3

we needed them
to be hopeless

born from boat parents
they have the nerve to imagine
it will all become better

but swimming in high levels
of unemployment
many can drown

beached
on the long dry stretch
of the hospitality industry
we invite them
to be called to exist

in the distance
a trigger

so begins the day

bring your bones here
every morning
and swim with them
for all the eyes
that we give an invitation

4

it sounds like you want
a more heartwarming enterprise
but community problems
aren't calling us

remember
all human development here
generally exists for profit

we don't change lives
we change attitudes

I chew up
the rhetoric of discipline
spit into their eyes
the force and objectives
of the home we know so well

before I cut
all the trouble out of them
I open the wound
for its smile

5

we've got another foot to scrub

who here can afford
to recognize
that we don't want to be convicted

we are targeting students
with a lot of unemployed shots
to meet their demands

now the dirty fundamentals
of executing this program
are probation and despondency

essentially we've agreed to
a dimension of losses
in commercial enterprise
with that awful surprise

the affordability
of consent

6

throw the vision out
the forced did its part

I'm starting lessons
at the eye level

my vocation now
is to introduce hospitality
as part of a
world history curriculum

it's a story about a room
and what's in it
waiting to be discovered
by a very serious criminal

if nobody's been convicted
then nobody is the problem

wake up

you sleep here
and you're gone

your identity
obscured
by the very long shadow
of a great historian

look for the door
he came in

wake up

BECOMING THE CANDIDATE

(This Is Not)   An Interview with the Managing Director of Luxury

1

my first lesson
was about the traditions of hospitality
and the social will to profit

they wanted us to cultivate
a good tone to this country

so making sure that we researched
all the uses of a face
we set about reading the syllabus
they fit inside
this beautiful beach ball

we touched the hearts and souls
of emotional distance

this is the type of connection
you stick to

hello people
beyond the reach

in the gardens you see yourself
the beautiful peacock
and the story of what he did

press next episode

2

someone always wants to go
the extra mile

the dollar rose with me
a star pupil that pays
attention to detail

for me the most important thing
is to provide service invisible
so sweet
that when it happens to you
you didn't even see it

I've lived on less
than these back bends

the finer things in life
get in the way

look in the game to stay in the game
empty

3

a great talent exists in this country

the beast in wool pants
about the old city
was my teacher

with a degree in
assessing and suppressing
prostitutes
he designed me
one year at a time

but very special leaders
also have beautiful tempers

you could find
your feet broken off
at the bottom
of the cliff

most learned how to persevere

the school toasted
each one of our souls
with the trading
of such severity

4

if you find yourself
in a room filled with nothing
that's when we can talk about it

the little refuge of the school uniform

I could explain
how small the practice is
of being in the Bahamas

the killers it hides in its midst
are really teachers
who preach the Bible
via law school dreams

poor little robot

you want to walk around
the ruins of the property
and you want to discover things
you want to see
you are a wonderful gentleman

but you are not
explorer people

your whole life
cooking in a prison
the ultimate rebrand
of this tropical rosary

5

the gifts that come
with this training period
are over

all I've learned
is how to be
frozen in time

a little story to focus on
while guests take nice
shits on the beach
of this nation

never considering
the fury surrounding those people
that attend to the everyday
brand promise

never conceding that
it's really about taking here

I want guests to take away
my memory
that fearful education of hospitality

steal the little moments
before dawn
when we catch glimpses of
the fool I've become
enduring the region
being executed on me

SIT DOWN AND TRY TO BE SOMEONE

(This Is Not)   An Interview with the Interior Designer

1

how wonderful
that at this kitchen table
people are seeking adventure
knowing that it will be
delivered to them

come in
do you see a menu for yourself
dinner was a roasted casino
the type of thing we pride ourselves on
lifestyle hotels were weeping
for a bite

are you interested in
our special
the entrée of common sense

eat up

I was raised on
this kind of home cooking

2

in the beginning
we were told hope
is the master plan

the mission had been to
lie in the hotel's arms
and try to figure out
what had happened

it was a hollow kind of thing
the words that we felt
but couldn't say

that's when we started eating

I sat on a guest
and added a dash of
glamour and stupidity
before I bit down

now we capture audiences
for sport
and it's open season

3

I consider myself
a citizen of the world

the city I remember once
is it you

raised
to get hit on
I refuse to
play with love stories

we're just creating excuses
so the guests will feel well
about their expiration date

this is the time
for alarm

you don't have to run

this oven
trimmed with the finest furnishings
China has to offer
is almost ready for you

4

our beds
spice sauces

can we collectively
get all of Bahamian history
into a recipe book

when you finally taste it
it will make you feel like
you're enjoying yourself more

come and see
what they're talking about

I'll make you appreciate
what you've always had

climb on top of me
split my casino

I'm in season
enjoy it

I want you
to come back often

you're enjoying yourself

THE DAY YOU GET TO CLUTCH

(This Is Not)   An Interview with the Vice President of Human Resources

1

light me up
I'm a fire
of different brands

each one of them
a unique technique
to catch people

to further my career
we are working
on my property

he wants me to invest
in hospitality
to get the technique down
between act and experience

can you stand the heat

at my age
how exciting
to be on course
so far from any other single
bright destiny of mine

2

it's our world
want to join

it's going to be
nothing
like we've seen before

you know what to wear
for the figure
of night

everyday he needs
an evening sound
on the floor

a tear of the skirt
will happen
at some point

it's he that finds
the best sunsets
around the world

that's how much
he brings to the table

he is opportunity
he is growth
and we have positions
available

3

in your career
your only hope
is to listen well
in a bikini

our work is to reckon with
the tides of
unsettled vacations

they beat us
to see
the smallest things
to get right
every single day

kicked again and again
you learn
to stay down
like your country

4

I know the cage
a few of us
can see it

lately
one of the things
we want
is to tear down
what we have been growing

this isn't a picnic

to be reminded
every day
you are nothing
on wet sheets
like you did your job
happy to come to work
with these beasts
who eat the light

5

time to declutter

set alight
all that I can see
to illuminate
for our visitors
a different environment
one where duty
sets the stage

each neck
commuting back
again and again
to come face to face
with death
and his wares
every single dark day

A HOMICIDE WE ALL KNOW WELL

(This Is Not)   An Interview with the Corporate Director of Destination Marketing

1

love is based on
what we have to offer

we're a great service

every guest who walks
into our soul
will be wowed

stylish and unique
we were designed to
fit the parameters of
of human desire

we embrace the culture
and feel a building
embrace back

touch a block
baby
and think of all the people
you ever loved

2

my background in hospitality
is that I lived in an empty castle
as a young child

tourism is like a bikini
made out of thick wool

I wonder if I'll ever get to
shine again

I do not want to fall from
my high hopes

the customer wants a need
so we are going to make this
the best estimation in the world

3

so what are you looking for

I redefine the game
and beat them with it
so they have something new
to come back to

I work on my knees
you'll get to choose
my passion

word of mouth is always
the best advertisement

just make me smile
he says

she says
all of you is
the deal

yes
he says
bleed

elevate our experiences

action

4

it is a phenomenal want
to continue the hum of being here

even the way I think
is a product

where can I go to vomit
into the air
taking with it every thought
I'm committed to

on the phone there are
flashbacks of my autonomy

I admit I was nearby
navigating to come back

I'm a compass
trying to find anywhere else in the world
where you really get nowhere

speak to how the hearts
of some sort of exciting place
return here again and again

people are always in love
the less they remember

5

what does it mean to buy
a world that's correct

the rich and famous playground
is basically a raid at our doorsteps

on the news tonight
police caught the hotels
trying to sell themselves

when did this accident
happen over and over again

an insulating smog of
pop culture
has been overwhelming
the sky

breathe it in
and listen for further instructions
on the radio stream

we'll soon embrace a war
over this ocean

with the blessing of the enemy
leave a prayer right here
at the locked door
of the kingdom

6

I'm going after
a different customer

I'm moving away
to be more real

before resigning
I want to talk
with a knife you have

split down
my western hemisphere
I am going into existence

you will notice me this time

I have warped into fire
fully engulfed and fully calm
a self-mocking bomb

I wake up to burn
the morning

I come to light the wooden bodies
with painted faces
drinking and singing in town

i'm going after a different customer

THE REST OF OUR LIFE IS NOT A POEM

(This Is Not)   An Interview with the Front Office Manager

1

I realize that a lot of people
see home as their future
a whole new beginning
to calm the salt
in their wounds

I was extremely humbled
to be selected
from the auction

our hero
is so kind to me
so kind

gosh
I was so excited to come home
and get a better story
for the rest of my life

2

                    I really love
                this commitment to
              being the right example

          I started off as an associate
                in the service industry
                             everyday
               an axle and an attitude

                       we were quiet
         put on the fast-paced smile
              so you didn't have to have
                          an answer
                   when a person
          asked a question we knew
                 but couldn't say

                           no pain
        would have that kind of face

3

you have to be committed
to walk the hall of your success

the promotion he described to me
was kind of a makeshift
public relations
just maintenance with diesel
honestly

I sing to the market
giving people
an opportunity to learn
that what is important for our times
is to exist within the lines

do re mi
I'm really enjoying being loved

I know that I had to work hard
to prove that I deserve this

4

dear sad people
of our nostalgia
I can tell you
what they don't tell us

I'm afraid
you have to love this country
but you also
have to be careful about
your love for this country

you have to love
everything about it
that can be expected

that's extremely important

because everything
they shout out
you have to own

5

it is tiring to keep up
this cool existence

what is your most
favorite place

my favorite is a hurricane

happy as she expands
touching land
singing
while she can get
almost every single place

a lot of people around me
are tumbling
very low on the ground
I can actually start collapsing

I find her starry eye
in the wall of water
and I'm home

you have to own everything

AUTHOR'S NOTE

These poems were created with text extracted from interviews run through a voice recognition software. The resulting distorted and fragmented language used to talk about building a resort development in The Bahamas felt closer to lived reality than any accurate transcription.

This is a work of satire. Names, characters, businesses, places, events, locales, and incidents are either the products of the author's imagination or used in a fictitious manner. Any resemblance to actual persons, living or dead, or actual events is purely coincidental.

ACKNOWLEDGEMENTS

I'm very grateful to the editors of the following publications who have generously shared previous versions of these poems: "The Overall Record for Being Human" in *The WomanSpeak Journal of Writing and Art* by Caribbean Women (Vol. 8, 2016) and "Becoming the Candidate: (This Is Not) An Interview with the Managing Director of Luxury"; "Sit Down and Try to Be Someone: (This Is Not) An Interview with the Interior Designer"; and "A Homicide We All Know Well: (This Is Not) An Interview with the Corporate Director of Destination Marketing" in *PREE* (Issue 2: Pressure, 2019). I'd also like to express my gratitude to the National Art Gallery of The Bahamas for facilitating and exhibiting some of these poems in my installation "Orientation" for NE7: Antillean in 2014; to The Bocas Literary Festival in Trinidad for giving me a platform to share and discuss several poems from this collection in 2016 during the reading "Poetry Is An Island;" and to BBC Radio 4 for including a reading of one of these poems on "Writing the new Caribbean: Under the Surface" in 2017.

Previous versions of two of these poems appeared in chapbooks: "The Overall Record for Being Human" was published by Poinciana Paper Press in 2015 with the encouragement of Antonius Roberts, and appeared in the exhibition "Tourists Only" at the Antonius Roberts Studio & Gallery at Hillside House during the 2015 Transforming Spaces Art Tour. "Now That I Change: (This Is Not) An Interview with the Managing Arts Director" was published by Current Books in 2018 and exhibited, along with a sound accompaniment, at The Current: Baha Mar Gallery and Art Center, during the 2018 exhibition "Pattern". I am very grateful to these two gallery spaces for intentionally making space for these publications and handling their installations and distribution in my absence.

A selection of these poems were completed during a writing residency in the summer of 2018 at The Current: Baha Mar Gallery and Art Center, kindly funded by a Summer Research Grant from The Gradate College at the University of Iowa.

Teamwork makes the dream work. These poems would not exist without The Current: Baha Mar Gallery and Art Center. Thank you John for allowing "your" interview to be the first poem—your early response gave me the audacity to keep going. Thank you Current 1.0 members—Cydne, Khia, Richardo, Piaget,

Nastassia, Rashad, Christina, and Alecia—for your humor, camaraderie, and sweet tunes during a strange time in all of our lives. Thank you to the present Current team members for supporting this project through my summer residency. I hope we all continue to use our positions to make space for necessary subversive conversations in an environment that actively tries to erase us every day.

Thank you to the marketing department for giving me the assignment that inspired this collection—ill-equipped in experience, hard-strapped for time, and taking it on for free, I must nevertheless apologize for its lateness and remind you of the risk when you hire and mistreat creative writers. Thank you Valentino and Karlyle for humoring me. Thank you, SDI, for having the self-awareness and courage to give Bahamian art space in a place where it has often not been welcome.

Thank you, Margot, fellow dark humor enthusiast, for being the first listener of these early drafts. Thank you, summer writing workshop crew—Yasmin, Letitia, Mae, Ide, and Natalie—for your thoughtful and critical feedback on many of these poems. Thank you, Leslie, for your "Hawkeye". Thank you Manfred for listening to me read every single new poem to you, in person or over the phone, as the collection finally came together. I still think that meeting you shortly after I stopped going into the office was the sign that my hardship was worth living through.

Thank you Julie, Sara L, Sara S, Karen, and Matt for your feedback on this project and its design—especially its design, especially during last minute requests, second guesses, small meltdowns, and missed deadlines.

Finally, as always, thank you to my parents Pia and John whose unconditional love means they support my work no matter how weird they think it is. Thanks for listening to me read one of the earliest drafts of a poem and telling me to keep going. Thank you for coming to my launches and readings and exhibitions and open studios. Thank you for the funding that allows me to make the books that I want my poems to live in and through. Thank you for instilling in me the value of integrity (and a good glass of wine at the end of the day) that sustained me through the summer of 2015. You were right: this too shall pass, and something will come of it.

Sonia Farmer is a writer, visual artist, and small press publisher who uses letterpress printing, bookbinding, hand-papermaking, and digital projects to build narratives about the Caribbean space. She is the founder of Poinciana Paper Press, a small and independent press located in Nassau, The Bahamas, which works with writers and artists using multiple forms of publishing to advance the diversity of narratives in Caribbean literature. Her artwork has been regionally and internationally exhibited and is included in multiple institutional and personal collections. She is the author of *Infidelities* (Poinciana Paper Press, 2017) which was longlisted for the 2018 OCM Bocas Prize for Caribbean Literature. She has also self-published several chapbooks. Her poetry won the 2011 Prize in the Small Axe Literary Competition and has appeared in various journals. She holds a BFA in Writing from Pratt Institute and an MFA in Book Arts from the University of Iowa.

www.ingramcontent.com/pod-product-compliance
Lightning Source LLC
Chambersburg PA
CBHW060424010526
44118CB00017B/2346